INJUSTICE

GODS AMONG US

VOLUME 2

INJU

GODS A

VOLU

THIS STORY TAKES PLACE BEFORE
THE START OF THE GAME

Tom Taylor
Writer

**Mike S. Miller   Bruno Redondo   Tom Derenick
Kevin Maguire   Neil Googe   Jheremy Raapack
Xermanico   Jonas Trindade**
Artists

**Rosemary Cheetham   Alejandro Sanchez
David Lopez & Santi Casas of Ikari Studio**
Colorists

Wes Abbott
Letterer

STICE
ONG US
E 2

SUPERMAN Created by JERRY SIEGEL and JOE SHUSTER.
By Special Arrangement with the Jerry Siegel Family.

BASED ON THE VIDEOGAME INJUSTICE: GODS AMONG US

Jim Chadwick Editor – Original Series
Aniz Ansari Assistant Editor – Original Series
Rachel Pinnelas Editor
Robbin Brosterman Design Director – Books
Louis Prandi Publication Design

Hank Kanalz Senior VP – Vertigo & Integrated Publishing

Diane Nelson President
Dan DiDio and Jim Lee Co-Publishers
Geoff Johns Chief Creative Officer
Amit Desai Senior VP – Marketing & Franchise
                          Management
Amy Genkins Senior VP – Business & Legal Affairs
Nairi Gardiner Senior VP – Finance
Jeff Boison VP – Publishing Planning
Mark Chiarello VP – Art Direction & Design
John Cunningham VP – Marketing
Terri Cunningham VP – Editorial Administration
Larry Ganem VP – Talent Relations & Services
Alison Gill Senior VP – Manufacturing & Operations
Jay Kogan VP – Business & Legal Affairs, Publishing
Jack Mahan VP – Business Affairs, Talent
Nick Napolitano VP – Manufacturing Administration
Sue Pohja VP – Book Sales
Fred Ruiz VP – Manufacturing Operations
Courtney Simmons Senior VP – Publicity
Bob Wayne Senior VP – Sales

INJUSTICE: GODS AMONG US VOLUME 2

Published by DC Comics. Compilation Copyright © 2015 DC Comics.
All Rights Reserved.

Originally published in single magazine form in INJUSTICE: GODS
AMONG US 7-12 and INJUSTICE: GODS AMONG US ANNUAL 1.
Copyright © 2013, 2014 DC Comics. All Rights Reserved.
All characters, their distinctive likenesses and related elements
featured in this publication are trademarks of DC Comics.
The stories, characters and incidents featured in this publication
are entirely fictional. DC Comics does not read or accept
unsolicited ideas, stories or artwork.

DC Comics, 1700 Broadway, New York, NY 10019
A Warner Bros. Entertainment Company.

Printed by RR Donnelley, Owensville, MO. USA. 12/5/14. First Printing.
ISBN: 978-1-4012-5045-4

Library of Congress Cataloging-in-Publication Data

Taylor, Tom, 1978- author.
    Injustice : Gods Among Us Volume 2 / Tom Taylor ; [illustrated by]
Mike S. Miller, Tom Derenick.
      pages cm
    ISBN 978-1-4012-5045-4
  1. Graphic novels. I. Miller, Mike S, illustrator. II. Derenick, Tom,
illustrator. III. Title. IV. Title: Gods Among Us, Volume 2.
    PN6727.T293I56 2014
    741.5'973—dc23
                                        2014010283

IT'S BEEN ONE MONTH.

ONE MONTH TO THE DAY SINCE A CALCULATED ACT OF MADNESS TOOK SO MANY LIVES.

NO ONE HAS SET FOOT IN THE CITY SINCE THAT DAY.

NO SOUND HAS BEEN HEARD IN THESE ONCE BUSTLING STREETS.

UNTIL NOW...

NOW, TWO WORDS— TWO IMPOSSIBLE WORDS—HAVE COME OUT OF THE RUINS.

ZZZzzz

ZZZ... I'M ALIVE... ZZ

14.95

ZZZ... I'M ALIVE... ZZZZZZ

...I'M ALIVE... ZZZZZZ

I'M ALIVE.

GREAT. A NARROW, CONFINED SPACE THAT LEADS DEEP UNDERGROUND.

THIS DOESN'T FEEL LIKE A TRAP AT ALL.

YOU STAND GUARD OUT HERE.

WHAT'S INSIDE?

I DON'T KNOW. I CAN'T SEE IN.

THIS IS WHERE THE SIGNAL'S COMING FROM. THAT TRANSMITTER ATTACHED TO THE DOOR.

IT MUST HAVE BEEN DAMAGED BY THE BLAST. IT'S A MIRACLE IT'S WORKING AT ALL.

OR SOMEONE WANTS US TO THINK THAT.

WHAT IS IT?

I'M NOT SURE...

...I FEEL LIKE WE'RE BEING WATCHED.

YOU WERE RIGHT. IT'S LUTHOR. HE'S ALIVE.

IF ANYONE COULD SURVIVE THAT, IT WOULD BE HIM. HOW?

HE HAD A SPEEDSTER ON THE PAYROLL. NOT SOMEONE ON FLASH'S LEVEL BUT STILL VERY FAST. THIS SPEEDSTER HAD ONE JOB. GET LUTHOR TO HIS BUNKER IN AN EVENT LIKE THIS.

WHAT HAPPENED TO THIS SPEEDSTER?

"AFTER SHE GOT LEX TO SAFETY, SHE WENT BACK OUT. LEX BELIEVES SHE TRIED TO SAVE PEOPLE--"

"--SHE WASN'T FAST ENOUGH."

I DIDN'T GET MUCH ELSE. WONDER WOMAN SENSED ME SOMEHOW.

BE CAREFUL OF DIANA. SHE DOESN'T SEEM HERSELF.

WHERE'S LEX LUTHOR NOW?

HI. I'M BILLY BATSON. I'M WONDERING IF YOU HAVE TIME TO ANSWER A QUESTION ABOUT THE SUPERHEROES?

IS THIS FOR SCHOOL OR SOMETHING?

SURE.

I JUST WANT TO KNOW HOW YOU FEEL ABOUT THE SUPERHEROES' RECENT ACTIONS. PUT SIMPLY, DO YOU THINK WHAT THEY'RE DOING IS RIGHT OR WRONG?

TOTALLY RIGHT! I THINK WHAT THEY'RE DOING IS AWESOME. I HEARD SUPERMAN PULLED THE JOKER'S STILL-BEATING HEART OUT OF HIS CHEST.

FATALITY!

I DON'T WANT TO COMMENT.

WHY?

WHAT IF THEY'RE LISTENING? THEY COULD BE LISTENING TO ME RIGHT NOW. THEY COULD BE WATCHING ME IN THE SHOWER.

SO, YOU'RE AFRAID OF THEM?

I SAID I DON'T WANT TO COMMENT.

I'M ALL FOR IT. I DON'T KNOW WHY IT'S TAKEN THEM THIS LONG. IT'S ABOUT TIME SOME OF THESE GUYS WERE PUT IN THEIR PLACE.

HEY, YOU OUT THERE. THE DAY WHEN YOU COULD MURDER PEOPLE OR OPPRESS THEM OR STARVE THEM WHILE YOU EAT BIG ARE OVER.

WHY?

WHY WHAT?

WHY ARE YOU DOING THIS?

"WHY ARE YOU ASKING THIS QUESTION?"

YESTERDAY

CYBORG, I'M NEARLY THERE. HAVE YOU AND FLASH LOCATED GL?

FLASH IS EVACUATING THE CITY AND--

DAMN IT!

HE'S DOWN!

I REPEAT-- GREEN LANTERN IS DOWN!

ANY SIGN OF HIS ATTACKER?

I CAN'T SEE A THING.

SUPERMAN?

NGG... NO.

HE GOT AWAY.

WAIT! SOMETHING'S APPROACHING FAST.

IS IT HIM?

IT BETTER BE.

BECAUSE, WHATEVER IT IS, I'M ABOUT TO BRING IT DOWN HARD.

THAT'S IT. FLY TOWARDS THE GIANT CANNON YOU STUPID MASS-MURDERING--

YOU'RE NOT WORRIED AT *ALL?* YOU DON'T THINK THEY'RE GOING TOO FAR?

ARE YOU KIDDING? I HOPE THEY HURRY UP WITH THE DESPOTIC RULERS AND GET BACK *HERE.*

START DEALING WITH ALL OF THOSE CORRUPT POLITICIANS WHO ARE JUST FRONTS FOR EVIL CORPORATIONS. LOCK UP SOME OF THE PEOPLE WHO ARE SUPPOSED TO BE REPRESENTING US, WHO ARE ACTUALLY DESTROYING OUR COUNTRY FOR THEIR OWN POLITICAL GAIN.

I'VE LIVED THROUGH THIS BEFORE. PEOPLE WHO HAVE RISEN UP AND SEIZED POWER FOR NOBLE REASONS.

IT ALWAYS STARTS WITH GOOD INTENTIONS AND SUCH HOPE.

I CAME TO THIS COUNTRY TO ESCAPE PEOPLE LIKE THIS, TO SEEK A BETTER LIFE.

I FOUND ONE.

BUT THESE BEINGS WOULD RULE THE WHOLE WORLD. THERE WOULD BE NO ESCAPE. THERE WOULD BE NO BETTER LIFE TO BE FOUND.

YOU SHOULD NOT HAVE STOOD IN THE WAY OF MY RETRIBUTION, HALF-MAN.

BLACK ADAM!

THOOM

TOOOY

CRICK

NAAARGH!!!

YOU'RE DONE, ADAM.

I AM *NOT* DONE. SOMEONE IN THIS CITY FIRED A SHELL INTO MY COUNTRY. THEY KILLED CHILDREN OF KAHNDAQ.

I AM KAHNDAQ'S LEADER, ITS PROTECTOR AND ITS WRATH. MY COUNTRY WILL SUFFER NO SUCH ATTACK WITHOUT VENGEANCE, SO LONG AS I HAVE POWER.

THEN WE WILL *TAKE* YOUR POWER.

WHAT ARE YOU DOING?

ASKING HIM A QUESTION.

SHAZAM, HOLD HIM.

KNOW THAT YOU CANNOT LIE WHILE TOUCHING THIS LASSO.

WONDER WOMAN, IF YOU COMPEL HIM TO SAY THE WORD...HE'S ANCIENT. I DON'T KNOW IF HE WILL SURVIVE THE TRANSFORMATION.

THEN ASK HIM IF THERE'S ANY OTHER WAY.

ADAM, TELL ME HOW CAN WE STOP YOU FROM KILLING AGAIN?

YOU CANNOT. I WILL KILL WITHOUT MERCY. I WILL SLAUGHTER *ANYONE* WHO WOULD THREATEN KAHNDAQ. I WILL TEAR WHOLE COUNTRIES APART!

AND KNOW THAT YOU ARE NO DIFFERENT TO ME. YOU ARE CHOOSING THE SAME PATH. YOUR END WILL BE THE SAME.

YOU WILL RULE. YOU WILL BRING ABOUT PEACE. BUT THEY WILL *FEAR* YOU.

BLACK ADAM--

BILLY! PROMISE ME.

--TELL US.

PROMISE ME THAT KAHNDAQ WILL BE SAFE!

WHAT IS YOUR MAGIC WORD?

SHAZAM!

HE'S ALIVE.

SH...
SH...

NO.

⟨IT'S ALL RIGHT. THE DANGER HAS PASSED.⟩

⟨PASSED? HOW? WE ARE SURROUNDED BY ANGRY, POWERFUL GODS WHO WOULD DECIDE OUR FUTURE.⟩

⟨I UNDERSTAND.⟩

⟨YOU **DON'T** UNDERSTAND. HOW COULD YOU? YOU ARE ONE OF THEM. GO BACK TO YOUR SKIES, ANGRY GOD. DO NOT PRETEND TO UNDERSTAND US.⟩

"BUT I **CAN** UNDERSTAND. AND MAYBE I'M THE ONLY ONE WHO CAN BECAUSE I **AM** ONE OF THEM MOST OF THE TIME--"

--SO I'VE BEEN ASKING AROUND. TRYING TO WORK OUT HOW OTHER PEOPLE ARE FEELING.

SHAZAM!

AND YOU'RE THE LAST PERSON I WANT TO ASK THIS QUESTION.

DO YOU THINK WHAT THEY'RE DOING IS RIGHT OR WRONG?

I CAN SEE THAT SUPERMAN AND WONDER WOMAN ARE DOING THIS FOR THE GREATER GOOD. THEY COULD BRING ABOUT REAL PEACE ON EARTH.

THAT SOUNDS LIKE THE WISDOM OF SOLOMON.

I DON'T HAVE THAT. I'M TWELVE.

SO, WHAT DO YOU SEE WITHOUT THE WISDOM OF SOLOMON?

I SEE EVERYTHING YOU SEE AND DO. I SAW THE FACES OF THOSE TERRIFIED ATLANTEANS. I HELD AQUAMAN'S THROAT WHEN ALL HE WAS TRYING TO DO WAS PROTECT HIS PEOPLE. I SAW THE BODIES IN THAT CITY AND THE TERRIFIED SURVIVORS. AND I HELD BLACK ADAM DOWN, NOT KNOWING IF HE WOULD DIE WHEN WE STRIPPED HIM OF HIS POWERS.

YOU THINK WHAT YOU'RE DOING IS RIGHT, AND MAYBE IT IS.

BUT I DON'T THINK SOMEONE AS YOUNG AS ME IS SUPPOSED TO SEE THIS STUFF...I THINK...I THINK IT'S AFFECTING ME.

AND MAYBE THAT ANSWERS MY QUESTION.

FIGHTING AND FAMINE HAVE LEFT OVER A MILLION PEOPLE DISPLACED IN MOGADISHU.

AND NOW, THE RAINY SEASON HAS COME.

A TENT MADE OF STICKS AND OLD CARDBOARD CAN'T STAND UP TO WIND AND POURING RAIN. AND, WITHOUT CLEAN WATER, MOSQUITO NETS AND SHELTER, THE PEOPLE CAN'T STAND UP TO THE DISEASES THAT THE FLOODS BRING.

IT'S TIME WE DID MORE.

MOST OF THE DISPLACED PEOPLE HERE ARE WOMEN. BUT IT'S THE MEN WHO CARRY GUNS.

TWO GENERATIONS OF MEN WHO HAVE GROWN UP WITH GUNS IN THEIR HANDS, WITHOUT COMMAND OR CONTROL.

IT'S THE SECURITY FORCES AND SOLDIERS, THE PEOPLE WHO ARE SUPPOSED TO PROTECT THESE CAMPS, THAT ARE CAUSING SO MUCH PAIN.

THAT CHANGES TONIGHT.

I CAN HEAR THE CRIES IN THE DARK.

THE FEAR.

THE VIOLENCE.

NIGHT AFTER NIGHT IT'S THE SAME IN OVER FIVE HUNDRED CAMPS ACROSS MOGADISHU. NO ONE EVER COMES TO THEIR AID.

Cover Art by Mico Suayan with David Lopez & Santi Casas of Ikari Studio

THE WATCHTOWER.

"BATMAN SIMPLY LET YOU GO?"

"NO, LEX. HE GAVE ME A MESSAGE. HE SAID HE DOESN'T WANT TO HAVE TO FIGHT US BUT WE HAVE TO STOP WHAT WE'RE DOING.

HE WANTS US TO STOP WORKING *FOR* THE WORLD AND START WORKING *WITH* IT.

MAYBE WE SHOULD CONSIDER WHAT BATMAN IS SAYING?

I AGREE. IT FEELS LIKE, EVER SINCE METROPOLIS, WE'VE BEEN REACTING. I'D LIKE TO SLOW DOWN AND TALK ABOUT WHAT WE'RE DOING HERE.

WHAT WE'RE *DOING* IS FINALLY BRINGING REAL PEACE TO OUR WORLD.

WHAT ABOUT THAT KID YOU CRIPPLED IN AUSTRALIA? IS HE AT PEACE? NO. THE POOR KID TRIED TO STAND UP FOR SOMETHING AND NOW HE'S EATING THROUGH A STRAW.

REALLY? WHAT ABOUT THE ATLANTEANS? DO YOU THINK THEY FEEL SAFER AFTER YOU ALL TOOK THEIR CITY AND DUMPED IT IN A DESERT?

UNPLEASANT THINGS HAVE TAKEN PLACE BUT MORE LIVES HAVE BEEN SAVED IN THESE LAST WEEKS THAN EVER BEFORE.

AT WHAT PRICE?

CRCK

KOOM

WONDER WOMAN!

BARRY.

I NEED TO TALK.

THIS CAN'T WAIT UNTIL *AFTER* THE PLANET-WIDE INVASION?

NO. AND THOUSANDS WILL DIE IN THE TIME IT TAKES TO TALK TO ANYONE ELSE.

KALIBAK SAID SOMETHING TO ME.

HE SAID I'D RATHER SPARE THE LIVES OF MY ENEMIES THAN SAVE THE LIVES OF MY PEOPLE.

WELL, LET'S NOT PUT TOO MUCH STOCK IN WHAT KALIBAK SAYS.

I THINK KALIBAK WAS RIGHT IN HIS OWN SICK WAY. THIS NEEDS TO CHANGE.

WHAT ARE YOU SUGGESTING?

BEING SANCTIMONIOUS AND ARROGANT DOESN'T MAKE YOU RIGHT, *BRUCE!*

THERE ARE PEOPLE IN THIS ROOM WHO DON'T KNOW YOUR SECRET IDENTITY, AREN'T THERE?

BRUCE?

'*BRUCE.*' STRIKING TERROR INTO THE HEARTS OF CRIMINALS!

YOU'VE ASKED THESE PEOPLE TO FIGHT WITH YOU AND YOU HAVEN'T EVEN TOLD THEM WHO YOU ARE?

THEY *KNOW* WHO I AM.

"CLARK WAS SO UPSET.

"AND THAT WAS THE DAY--

"--THE DAY WE FIRST DISCOVERED WHAT CLARK CAN DO."

YOU'RE SAYING SUPERMAN IS A SCARED CHILD?

AREN'T WE ALL?

WE COULD DO IT, YOU AND I, COULDN'T WE?

IN WHAT? A DAY? TWO?

WE COULD NEVER GET RID OF ALL GUNS.

NO. BUT MOST. WE COULD DO IT.

YES.

CHECKMATE.

BUT JUST BECAUSE WE CAN DO IT, DOESN'T MEAN WE SHOULD.

UNLESS THEY GIVE UP THEIR GUNS WILLINGLY, THEY WILL RESENT US.

YES. BUT THEY WILL BE ALIVE TO RESENT US.

I KNOW.

THEY WILL RISE AGAINST US.

MAYBE. AND LET THEM COME AT US WITH STICKS.

BUT I FEAR HE WILL PUT THE WHOLE WORLD IN A FORTRESS TO KEEP IT SAFE.

WHAT WOULD YOU HAVE ME DO?

WHEN THE TIME COMES, I EXPECT YOU TO DO WHAT IS *RIGHT*.

YOU'VE JUST CREATED THE MEANS TO STOP HIM. YOU'VE CREATED SOMETHING THAT WILL PUT POWER IN ORDINARY HANDS, AND DON'T PRETEND FOR A SECOND THAT IT HASN'T OCCURRED TO YOU.

"I FEAR A DAY MAY COME WHEN THE WORLD NEEDS TO BE SAVED FROM OUR SON.

"ALL I ASK IS THAT, ON THAT DAY--

"--YOU FIND A WAY TO SAVE HIM TOO."

ESSENTIALLY, WE'RE TALKING ABOUT A TECHNOLOGY THAT WILL ENHANCE THE STRENGTH AND DURABILITY OF ORDINARY PEOPLE A THOUSAND-FOLD.

MAGIC PILLS? REALLY?

IT'S NOT MAGIC. IT'S SOMETHING SUPERMAN AND I HAVE DISCUSSED FOR YEARS.

I JUST COULDN'T WORK OUT HOW TO REVERSE-ENGINEER THE KRYPTONIAN NANOTECHNOLOGY.

YEAH. I'M STILL ONLY HEARING 'MAGIC PILLS.'

YOU'RE SITTING ON A SPACE STATION HIGH ABOVE THE EARTH WITH MEN AND WOMEN WHO CAN LITERALLY MOVE MOUNTAINS AND YOU HAVE A PROBLEM WITH MAGIC PILLS?

I'M SURE THERE ARE ORDINARY PEOPLE IN ALL OF OUR LIVES WE WOULD TRUST WITH SUCH POWER.

I SUGGEST WE DRAW UP A LIST OF CANDIDATES.

IF WE HAD MORE PEOPLE WHEN APOKOLIPS ATTACKED, THINK OF HOW MANY LIVES WOULD HAVE BEEN SAVED.

WE NEED PEOPLE ON THE GROUND AT ALL TIMES.

OR ALL OF OUR GOOD WORK COULD BE UNDONE.

SO, YOU WANT A SUPERPOWERED ARMY?

NOT AN ARMY, GREEN LANTERN, A PEACE KEEPING FORCE. YOU OF ALL PEOPLE SHOULD UNDERSTAND THIS.

I'M SURE THERE ARE MANY WORLD GOVERNMENTS WHO WON'T SEE IT THAT WAY.

WHAT IF IT FELL INTO THE WRONG HANDS...?

YOU WANT US TO ASK OUR FRIENDS TO HELP POLICE THE WORLD?

IT WON'T. AND THIS TECHNOLOGY ISN'T JUST ABOUT PROTECTING THE WORLD, HAWKGIRL. IT'S ALSO ABOUT PROTECTING YOU.

"--IT WILL MAKE ALL OF YOU STRONGER."

TELEPORTER
DESTINATION: GOTHAM CITY

TK
TK

TELEPORTER
DESTINATION: GOTHAM C

HMM.

--LET GO!

UNF!

NO...

KSSSH

ALFRED!

ALFRED!

I'M SORRY... I DIDN'T KNOW HOW STRONG I WAS.

BRUCE...

WHERE'S BRUCE??

HNNGG.

I THINK WE SHOULD GO BACK TO THE WATCHTOWER, ROBIN.

NO. LEAVE HIM.

SINCE WHEN DO YOU LISTEN TO BATMAN, HAWKGIRL?

WAIT. WHAT ARE YOU DOING HERE? HOW DO YOU EVEN KNOW WHERE THE CAVE IS?

AFTER HE TOOK YOU. YOU CAME BACK. YOU CAME BACK AND YOU GAVE US HIS MESSAGE.

EVEN TODAY. YOU KEPT RAISING DOUBTS OVER THE PILL.

AND THE PENNY...

HAWKGIRL IS STRONG--

--BUT NOT THAT STRONG.

CLCK

YOU DON'T KNOW MY FATHER LIKE I DO... AND I BARELY KNOW HIM AT ALL.

NO ONE DOES.

HE WILL GO TO ANY LENGTHS.

I'VE SEEN THE FILES HE HAS ON EVERY ONE OF YOU, ON ALL OF THE JUSTICE LEAGUE. IT'S NOT JUST STRENGTHS AND WEAKNESSES. THOSE FILES INCLUDE YOUR PAST. YOUR FRIENDS. YOUR FAMILIES.

IF HE FEELS HE NEEDS TO, HE WILL USE THEM AGAINST YOU.

HE WILL STRIKE PREEMPTIVELY.

WE NEED TO BRING EVERYONE ELSE IN. GREEN LANTERN, RAVEN, SHAZAM. NO ONE SHOULD BE OPERATING ALONE.

WE NEED A PLAN IN PLACE TO PROTECT OTHERS CLOSE TO US.

THAT'S WHAT HE'LL BE COUNTING ON.

HE WANTS US TO REACT TO HIM. TO PULL BACK. TO GO ON THE DEFENSIVE.

HE'S ALWAYS THE ONE IN CHARGE OF ANY SITUATION, THE ONE WITH ALL OF THE KNOWLEDGE AND THE SMUG SUPERIORITY. BATMAN, ALWAYS PREPARED FOR ANYTHING.

NOT THIS TIME.

CYBORG, THE EMERGENCY BROADCAST SYSTEM. ALL DEVICES.

WHERE?

EVERYWHERE.

PEOPLE OF EARTH.

WE HAVE BEEN BETRAYED.

THE HERO KNOWN AS BATMAN HAS TAKEN ONE OF OUR PEOPLE. ONE OF YOUR HEROES.

HAWKGIRL HAS BEEN ABDUCTED.

AN IMPOSTER WAS PUT IN HER PLACE.

WAIT. WHAT?

BATMAN'S SPY HAS BEEN AMONG US FOR A WEEK.

SOMEWHERE, HAWKGIRL HAS BEEN HELD, NO DOUBT HOPING FOR RESCUE, AND WE, HER FRIENDS, DIDN'T EVEN KNOW SHE WAS MISSING.

BATMAN LIED AND KIDNAPPED TO GET WHAT HE WANTED.

NO MORE.

HE HAS TAKEN ONE OF OUR FRIENDS AND ALLIES, AND I AM TAKING SOMETHING OF HIS.

I AM TAKING HIS ANONYMITY.

DAMN YOU, CLARK.

PROTOCOL ICARUS.

BATMAN'S TRUE IDENTITY IS--

CSSHHHHH

CSSHHHH

CSSHHHHH

ANY IDEA WHAT'S HAPPENING?

NOPE.

WHATEVER IT IS, I'M GUESSING IT'S GOING TO SUCK.

YEP.

PROTOCOL ICARUS

PROTOCOL ICARUS

NO.

WHAT DO YOU MEAN, 'NO'?

HE WANTS OUR HANDS FULL. HE WANTS HIS IDENTITY. HE'S BUYING TIME SO THAT HE CAN PUT SOME CONTINGENCY PLAN IN PLACE.

I'M NOT GIVING HIM THAT TIME. LET ME FINISH ADDRESSING THE EARTH.

THE WATCHTOWER DOESN'T HAVE POWER. COMMUNICATIONS ARE OUT.

YOU'RE A LIVING COMPUTER--

--AND YOU'RE SUPPOSED TO BE THE SMARTEST MAN IN THE WORLD.

YOU'RE TELLING ME WE CAN'T PUT FOUR LITTLE WORDS ONLINE?

<<SuddenWick: Bruce Wayne dresses up like a bat?

<<TDerToy: Holy Crap. #BatmanisBruceWayne

<<TomTaylorRite: I know. #BatmanisBruceWayne

<<Superbigfan: Damn! #BatmanisBruceWayne

<<loisandjimmy: I knew already. #BatmanisBruceW

<Supermanfan: Weren't Batman and Catwoman a thing? That means...

BATMANisBRUCEWAYNE

⌘BATMAN

⌘BRUCEWAYNE

⌘WAYNE

⌘SUPERMAN

⌘BRUCE

GO SLOW. WE'RE NOT RUNNING OUT OF OXYGEN IN HERE ANYTIME SOON, AND I'D LIKE TO GET US BACK UP THERE QUICKLY ONCE I WORK OUT HOW BATMAN DID THIS TO US.

BURN ME!!!

NAAARGH!

AAARGHH!!

HE... HE WOULD HAVE...

I KNOW.

WHEN I WAS TWELVE YEARS OLD, I FELL OFF MY BIKE.

I DIDN'T JUST FALL OFF. IT WAS A BIT MORE SPECTACULAR THAN THAT. I WAS SPEEDING DOWN THE HILL AT IVE'S RESERVE OUTSIDE METROPOLIS. IT WAS A RIDICULOUSLY STEEP HILL.

IT WAS A STUPID THING TO DO BUT I WAS TWELVE, SO I WAS INDESTRUCTIBLE.

UNTIL I WASN'T.

I STILL REMEMBER IT...

THAT SECOND WHEN I WAS AIRBORNE.

THAT MOMENT WHEN I REALIZED JUST HOW MUCH IT WAS GOING TO HURT.

THEN A FACE FULL OF GRASS AND DIRT AND TEARS.

HNGG!

AND AN IMPOSSIBLE VOICE...

EXCUSE ME--

I MISS SUPERMAN.

I MISS THE GUY WHO ACTUALLY INSPIRED PEOPLE.

THE SUPERMAN WHO HAD TIME TO HELP A KID WHO FELL OFF A BIKE.

JAMES. GOOD TO GO?

YEAH. SURE.

BEFORE HE WAS CHANGED. BEFORE HE GRITTED HIS TEETH AND LOOKED ANGRY ALL THE TIME.

BEFORE HE BECAME ALL HARD AND DARK BECAUSE PEOPLE, SUPPOSEDLY, NEEDED HIM TO.

I MISS THE CITY OF TOMORROW--

--AND THE MAN OF YESTERDAY.

"...I THINK IT'S A MOTORBIKE."

WE NEED TO TAKE A LITTLE TRIP AGAIN?

WHUT'S THAT?

IT'S NOTHING.

THAT'S CRAP. NOTHIN' DOESN'T FLOAT INNA SPECIAL BOX.

I WANT IT.

IT WOULDN'T AFFECT YOU.

WHY? WHAT'S IT S'POSED TA DO?

THE PILLS ARE DESIGNED TO INCREASE THE STRENGTH AND DURABILITY OF A REGULAR PERSON.

SO, WHAT HAPPENS IF I TAKE ONE?

YOUR STRENGTH LEVELS ARE INCREDIBLY HIGH ALREADY. I'M NOT SURE IT WOULD--

MAYBE IT DOES NOTHIN'. MAYBE I GET TA HEAD BUTT A MOON IN HALF. I WANT ONE.

THERE'S BEEN VERY LITTLE TESTING DONE.

YOU WANT ME ON TH' JOB? I WANT ONE OF YER SUPER PILLS AS PAYMENT UP FRONT.

IT IS HIGHLY UNLIKELY IT WILL CHANGE HIS PHYSIOLOGY AT ALL.

FINE. YOU CAN HAVE ONE OF THE PILLS.

CAN YOU GET QUINN'S SCENT OFF OF THE CLOTHING?

YEP. SHE SMELLS NUTS.

YOU CAN'T POSSIBLY SPEAK TO HER SANITY BASED ON THE SCENT OF AN OLD PIECE OF CLOTHING.

DON'T QUESTION TH' MAIN MAN'S POWER. TH' SMELL OF CRAZY. IT DON'T WASH AWAY EASY.

I CAN SMELL ALL SORTS A THINGS.

AN' YOU SMELL NERVOUS. WHA'S TH' MATTER? YA GOT SOMETHIN' TA HIDE?

QUINN WAS LAST SEEN IN GOTHAM. I'D START THERE IF I WERE YOU.

I WANT HER ALIVE, LOBO. THERE'S TO BE NO COLLATERAL DAMAGE AND NO CIVILIAN DEATHS.

YOU'RE TAKIN' ALL TH' FUN OUTTA THIS.

DO YOU REALLY THINK IT'S WISE TO LET HIM LOOSE ON THE WORLD?

I HAVEN'T LET HIM LOOSE. HE'S WORKING WITHIN MY PARAMETERS. HE KNOWS WHAT I CAN DO IF HE STEPS OUT OF LINE.

AND I WANT HARLEY QUINN--

BZZZT

PRIVATE

BZZZT

ONLY THREE PEOPLE HAVE THIS PHONE NUMBER.

I KNOW, MISTER PRESIDENT. BUT WHAT YOU DO IN YOUR PRIVATE LIFE DOESN'T CONCERN ME.

WE HAVE A SITUATION AND I NEED A DISTRACTION.

HOW BIG A DISTRACTION?

I SEE.

THIS IS THE ADDRESS.

IT'S A UNISEX RESTROOM.

APPARENTLY.

SERIOUSLY, HOW MANY OF THESE SECRET HIDEOUTS DOES HE HAVE?

I'M GUESSING THAT'S A SECRET.

WHAT DID HE GIVE YOU?

I JUST HAVE THE NUMBER THREE.

HE TRUSTED ME WITH ONE NUMBER. HE TRUSTED YOU WITH A WHOLE ADDRESS. YOU EVER GOING TO TELL ME EXACTLY HOW YOU KNEW HE WAS BRUCE WAYNE?

NOT WHEN I CAN SEE HOW MUCH IT'S TORTURING YOU NOT KNOWING.

SO, DOOR THREE?

I GUESS.

WOULDN'T BE THE FIRST TIME YOU AND I HAVE SNUCK INTO A RESTROOM CUBICLE TOGETHER.

SCAN COMPLETE.

WHAT THE HELL?

GREEN ARROW AND BLACK CANARY IDENTIFIED.

PLEASE PREPARE FOR RETINAL SCAN.

RETINAL SCAN COMPLETE. GREEN ARROW CONFIRMED.

RETINAL SCAN COMPLETE. BLACK CANARY CONFIRMED.

I DON'T KNOW WHAT SCARES ME MORE, THE FACT THAT HE HAS OUR EYES ON FILE OR THAT THE TOILET IS TALKING.

ELEVATOR INITIATED. PLEASE STAND CLEAR OF THE WALLS.

GREAT. ELEVATOR TOILET. THIS IS THE LEAST CLASSY SECRET HIDEOUT EVER.

THE NORTH POLE.

WE'RE HALF A MILE AWAY FROM THE FORTRESS.

ATOM, TAKE CATWOMAN AHEAD SO SHE CAN START FINDING US A WAY INSIDE.

THERE'S NO WAY THE WARSHIP MOVEMENT COULD BE MISSED BY SUPERMAN AND THE LEAGUE.

"THEY SHOULD BE IN KOREA BY NOW."

150

ANYTHING?

NOTHING AT ALL, CAPTAIN.

WHERE ARE THEY?

SUPERMAN. IS THERE A PROBLEM?

I DON'T WANT TO WASTE MY TIME MAKING THOSE SHIPS TURN AROUND WHEN YOU CAN DO IT WITH ONE PHONE CALL.

YOU CAN'T COME HERE AND--

YES. I CAN.

WHY ARE YOU DOING THIS? YOU MUST HAVE KNOWN THAT I WOULDN'T LET THIS STAND.

YOU *DID* KNOW.

YOU WANTED ME DISTRACTED IN KOREA. WHY? WHAT ARE YOU--?

NO.

GET BACK!

MOVE!

OLLIE!

I'M OKAY, PRETTY BIRD.

STAND BACK.

NO. YOUR SCREAM COULD BRING DOWN MORE OF THE ROOF.

DINAH. WE HAVE TO GO. IF WE'RE STILL HERE WHEN SUPERMAN COMES BACK...

I'M NOT LEAVING HIM.

REMEMBER EARLIER WHEN YOU WERE TELLING US OFF FOR BICKERING WHILE SOMEONE WAS BUYING US A SMALL WINDOW OF TIME?

THAT WAS DIFFERENT. THAT WAS JUST THE FATE OF THE WORLD. THIS IS MORE IMPORTANT.

ARROW. I HID A LOCATOR INSIDE YOUR HOOD!

OF COURSE YOU DID...

KEEP SAFE AND KEEP THAT LOCATOR ON. TRY TO FIND ANOTHER WAY OUT. I PROMISE WE'LL COME BACK FOR YOU ONCE SUPERMAN HAS GONE.

DO YOU UNDERSTAND?

I HAVE MORE POWER IN ME THAN TEN NUCLEAR BOMBS, AND YOU AND YOUR STUPID MAGIC SWORD HAVE JUST BREACHED THE THING THAT CONTAINS IT.

NOW I HAVE A CHOICE TO MAKE. I CAN STAND HERE. I CAN LET GO. I CAN TAKE YOU AND THE ENTIRE NORTH POLE WITH ME.

OR I CAN DO WHAT'S RIGHT.

DO YOU REMEMBER, SUPERMAN? DO YOU REMEMBER WHEN YOU THOUGHT OF ANYONE OTHER THAN YOURSELF?

WHAT HAPPENED?

THEY... THEY TRIED TO KILL ME.

WHO?

CAPTAIN ATOM, WORKING WITH THE U.S. GOVERNMENT... AND BATMAN.

I'M SORRY. I...I DIDN'T KNOW BATMAN WAS CAPABLE OF THIS. I DIDN'T WANT TO BELIEVE.

I KNOW.

HNNG...

SHE'S STABLE BUT SHE NEEDS MEDICAL ATTENTION.

YOU NEED TO BE LOOKED AT, TOO.

ONCE I KNOW MY PARENTS ARE SAFE. NOT BEFORE.

GO.

KOOOM

HE'S HERE.

GET AWAY FROM THEM.

THINK, OLLIE.

CLARK, MY GOD. WHAT HAPPENED TO YOU?

THE U.S. GOVERNMENT JUST ORDERED MY DEATH. DO YOU KNOW ANYTHING ABOUT THAT, OLLIE?

I KNOW VERY LITTLE ABOUT ANYTHING. I DIDN'T EVEN KNOW WE WERE COMING HERE.

HELL, WE CAME TO THE NORTH POLE AND BLACK CANARY WORE FISHNETS.

THAT SHOWS A DISTINCT LACK OF PLANNING.

THINK!

SO, THESE ARE YOUR SUPER PILLS.

THIS IS IT, ISN'T IT? THE TECH YOU WERE AFTER? OLLIE SAVED THE DAY.

YES.

WE'LL WAIT BY THE TELEPORTER. HE MAY STILL--

NO.

HE'S NOT COMING.

I'M SORRY.

BRUCE! NO. DON'T--

FSSSSSS

SHE WON'T FORGIVE YOU FOR THIS, YOU KNOW.

I KNOW.

SHE CAN BE PISSED OFF AND *ALIVE*.

HIDE. ALL OF YOU. GO DEEP UNDERGROUND. IF THIS WORKS, I'LL FIND YOU.

Injustice #12 DC Collectibles Variant Cover